Dividing by Zero

Dividing by Zero

Barry Marks

Dividing by Zero

Copyright, 2015, Barry Marks
All Rights Reserved.

ISBN 978-0-9425-4491-6
Library of Congress Control Number: 2014937569

Cover and Interior Design by Megan Cary

Published by
Negative Capability Press
62 Ridgelawn Drive East
Mobile, Al. 36608

www.negativecapabilitypress.org

Writers are people who live inside their own heads and rail against the scenery. A poet would rather sit alone in a dark room and write about being lonely than go out and make a friend. Most of us are easy people to ignore and tough people to love.

For my parents and my children.

I'm sorry.

B.S.M.

Foreword

The book within this book is a daughter's compilation of her father's writings, together with some of her own. It is about her relationship with him and his with the world. It begins on a page containing the opening to his autobiographical narrative, one of his poems and, in the margin, her own story. It continues with each page containing one or more of his narrative and poems and her narrative, stories and poem.

None of the characters in this book bear significant resemblance to any real person. None of the events described, or anything like them, really happened.

It is a true story.

Dividing by Zero
A Family Memoir in Poetry, Fiction and Journal

by L. Shopinski

**When Asked What I Think about Death
I Remember the Truck**

> *…you will become a deer, torn in half
> by the engine it did not understand*
>   *Sherman Alexie*
>   "When Asked What I Think About
>   Indian Reservations, I Remember
>   A Deer Story"

That deer crushed beneath
the wheels of a logging truck
does not understand internal combustion engines
or even the simple tool,
the wheel of its death,
driven by the wheels, belts and cogs
of the metal machine that ends the machine
that is the deer.

But no, I think it is not
engine, truck, or wheel
but death that kills the deer.

And death that killed Custer and Crazy Horse,
my mother and my uncle,
death coming up behind me now
closer than it appears,
death that I do not understand
or I could outrun it, outdrive it,
shut it down.
But I cannot do any of these
because I do not understand the architecture,
the design, the internal combustion of death

even though every now and then
I think I hear its engine whine;
even though every now and then
death sounds its terrible horn.

                                    – Raymond Shaw
                                         2/24/12

How can you describe a life? What camera can capture pain, longing, joy? Loneliness in its many forms? He was always a poet, at least to me. I knew him by his pet sayings and figures of speech, the doggerel in the birthday cards, what I saw in his eyes. Or thought I saw. I never understood him, only that I was alone in his presence. The day we found him was the first time we read his poetry. It was the first time we saw the other writing. It was the day I found him.

I mourn the man I never knew. And I knew him more than anyone. Probably more than he allowed himself to know himself.

This is for you, Dad. And for me.

L.

I am writing to explain myself.
I cannot explain myself.

+

Let's face it. It's fun to be crazy. People are always saying, "I don't know, I guess I'm just crazy!" Like it's some kind of excuse. It's cool to be crazy. America loves the out-rage-ous. It's sexy. It's funny. It's

All the Robin Hoods Meet in Sherwood Forest

They toast one another with huge flagons while
all the Little Johns merrily bash each other with staffs
and compare their bigness to see whose
Little John-edness is most ironic.

The Friar Tucks tell each other dirty jokes
as the Will Scarlets compare doublets and tights
while the Alan-A-Dales sing in disharmony
the glories of their respective Robins.

Once the toasting is done,
Errol Flynn and Douglas Fairbanks
scale treetops, daring one another to climb higher.
Kevin Costner arm-wrestles Russell Crowe (and loses),
Cary Elwes thrusts at Disney's animated fox-Robin as
Sean Connery and Richard Green take it all in
with that cool reserve reserved for real Brits.
A dozen or so lesser Robins wander about,
intent on proving themselves if
Claude Rains, Basil Rathbone, Alan Rickman,
or any other Sheriff of Nottingham,
Guy of Gisbourne or King John
would just cooperate.

A dozen assorted Maid Marions,
whose names are ironic as the Little Johns',
chat beneath the largest, noblest oak.

Dear Dad:
I had the dream again last night. The therapist says it is the same one even though the circumstances and faces change. Aunt Sarah said she had the same dream when you were kids and sometimes still does. Isn't that funny? Her therapist says it is because grandpa was always working and had such a bad temper that no one wanted to talk to him. She said grandpa worked sixteen hour days six days a week and he slept Sundays. No wonder we never saw him when we were growing up. He cried at your funeral, which actually surprised everyone. Neither of you cried when cancer took grandma, did you?

The dream is simple enough: something or someone is threatening the family. I am the one who saves us. Sometimes I fail. Sometimes I succeed. Most times I wake up too soon to tell. Sometimes I dream that you are there to hold me and tell me it will be all right. You say you love me and you wait long enough for me to say it back to you. If a dream is so good that you are sad when you wake is it a nightmare?

A mere blink away,
Wyatt Earps and Doc Hollidays
stride across Tombstone to their OK Corrals,
Burt Lancaster with his Kirk Douglas facing off
against Kurt Russell and his Val Kilmer, and
Kevin Costner (again) with his Dennis Quaid,
all those B Movie guys (not to mention Hugh O'Brien)
yanking out their Buntline Specials
and having at it for hero supremacy.

Tarzans, Counts Dracula, Supermen,
Batmen, Long John Silvers, Ebenezer Scrooges,
we could go on.
I often do.

Crazy. It's even more fun inside your own mind. It's liberating. When you are crazy it doesn't matter if you forget your keys. If you didn't like the Beatles OR Elvis OR Nirvana and now you don't care for Jay-Z or Mumford & Sons. If you don't like chocolate ice cream, geek-styled clothing, pro football, college football, Louis C.K., your family. You can keep yourself entertained for hours, even if the cable is out.

When you're crazy you like it inside yourself so much you stay there. Or at least the door is open to get back any time the conversation lags or the car won't start. Who needs Syfy or the Comedy Channel? Admittedly, it can get a little lonely, but you can always make a new friend.

Ode to My Daughter's Cat

Richard Parker is jumping on the bed Richard Parker
Richard Parker Richard Parker Richard Parker is
jumping on the bed where I am trying to sleep
I am trying to sleep Richard Parker Richard
Parker is jumping on the bed purring like
an insidious machine making himself
oh so comfortable Richard Parker's
purring machine in my legs and
I am trying to sleep I have said
goodnight and night was to be
what it is night should be all
all of it should be night but
it is not night it is not good
it is Richard Parker and
his insidious purring
machine and
everything is
Richard
Parker
every-
thing
is not
night
no
ev-
ery-
thing
is
Cat   Cat   Cat

It's fun to be crazy. It is not so much fun to be insane. Insane isn't cool. Insane is the opposite of liberating. Insane hides that sharp edge that slashes at the funny. It grabs at you just when you think you are doing so well. It won't shut up when the lights are off, even if your body has company. You don't shrug at people and say, "Maybe I suffer from a disassociation disorder." It is even less fun to try to remember how you got there. Especially when you can't quite get it straight.

when it rains * I feel the silver bullet * work its way deeper * and I * wolf * turn upon those I would love * for holding my feet * to the earth * and I * human being * pure of heart * who says his prayers by night * dream of the one * woman I love * and other things * that I cannot have * and I * being human * wake because * this is too much to dream

I Remember The Angel Made Me Forget

Take off your clothes and lie with me
so I will remember that I am alive
and forget that I will die.

I remember dimetrodons,
Mastodons, iguanodons,
the moment I first saw you naked,
the beginning of time.

I remember the Big Bang,
the Hindenberg, Jericho,
the moment my parents came together;
and I remember the supernova that will end it all,
the last breath I will take.

Oh, of course I recall
my red rocking horse,
my black tricycle, my blue bicycle,
the day I wet my brown shorts,
all that the mind collects and recollects.

I forget where I parked my car,
your birthday,
my sister's birthday (I think it was last month),
but I remember the moment
the angel tapped his finger on my lip
and I forgot everything I knew
because I forget what is in my brain.
What I remember
I remember in my bones.

I don't know when I began writing short stories. I think I began writing when I began thinking. Children are born imagining. That is why we have nightmares. It is also why we have dreams in which everything is wonderful and we can become princesses or good witches. Or simply happy wives and good mothers.

It would make more sense if we were Norwegian or something. Cold people. People who find it hard to say I love you or anything else because their jaws are frozen in a scowl. That might make sense. You're Jewish. So am I, more or less. Most of the dads I knew from Temple were excitable, touchy-feely. Warm. Not you. I thought you would have made a good Norwegian.

I Can't Help It

When I hear *trollop*,
I don't think of
slattern.
A slattern sounds dirtier,
lopsided somehow,
slovenly,
not at all like a *strumpet*.

Who would want anything to do
with a strumpet?
Sounds like someone sharp
and loud too.
At least a slattern wouldn't be much trouble,
but she wouldn't be as much fun as a *floozy*.

A floozy would be someone with
fruit-shaped earrings and long, long plastic
beads, lots of lipstick and frizzy red hair.
Not at all classy like a *mistress*.

Oh my, that sounds like
an expensive proposition.

Not free like a *tramp*,
who is easily dismissed
as a single-syllable error of judgment,
unlike a *harlot*

who would seem to carry
biblical implications or a *hussy*,
who doesn't seem like anyone I would
ever meet, although my wife might
think I know several, just as she might
accuse me of going *wenching*,
which sounds like a whale of a good time.

Any woman who can be verbed is my kinda gal
and a wench sounds satisfying,
as does a *tart,* who is apparently
a tasty *petit four,* but not a substantial confection
like a *trollop* whose ample-bottomed self
would dance into my dreams
and settle down like whipped cream

upon me
a *dude* (without chaps),
a pink-suited *playah,*
loafing *Lothario,*
smooth operator,
swinger, reprobate-roué-rake
more *lady's man* than *lady-killer* and *lover*
oh Lover Lover Lover come back to me
whatever your *nom d'amour* might be.

How do you love a wall? You convince yourself it is made of glass and that you are seeing through to the other side. That there is something there that is loving, caring, and hurting just as much as you are. You convince yourself that this is just the way life is and that you share everything you feel with the wall. This works even though the wall makes you see yourself, hazy and pale next to the real person on the other side.

Let me get down to what I want to say:
I was first molested when I was eight. It's true.
You don't want it to be. You want this to be something else. You don't want it to be me, the guy who is writing this telling you that he was molested at a young age. You want this to be said by a fictional character. You want it to be a metaphor.
Don't you?

It's true.
When I was eight I was sexually abused and it changed everything.

**Watching a Nature Show
I Get Close To My Inner Mammal**

I root for the hawk to get the snake, but
I never want to see the hawk get the meerkat.
Who could root against a meerkat?
I generally don't favor reptiles and such,
except baby turtles rushing to the surf
with Stuka-like seagulls picking them off.

I don't like seagulls,
except when they are up against fish.
I really have no sympathy for fish,
except maybe when the tiny ones
run afoul of crabs, mantis shrimp,
or those weird oversized spiders.

Mammal-on-mammal
murder is harder.
I marvel as the cheetah runs down the gazelle.
The ground flashes beneath my feet and I am *cat,*
until I see that soft eye staring at the camera
as the head lolls back and the soul of the
gazelle, or whatever they have under
the fur and antlers, departs.

Of course, when the cheetah brings its kill
home to its cubs, all is forgiven and I become
a big cat-guy all over again.

Only two things are consistent:
I can never understand
how the men behind the cameras
stay behind the cameras
when babies of every species
are run down, clawed, bitten, strangled and
swallowed whole or in pieces.
And no matter what the predator or prey,
I never root for snakes

Dad, I never told you what happened to me. You know I could never tell Mom. It would have become about her and about what she didn't do and how it hurt her. I love Mom. I thought about telling her. I never thought about telling you. Later on, I thought she held it against me, even before she knew. That was after I got old enough to be a person. A *mensch* we call it; a responsible adult person. Whenever she wanted me to do something she said "Be a *mensch.*" And she hated that I was one. Even before you left, she hated a lot of things. You never interfered with my relationship with Mom. You never protected me from her, either.

You never came into my room late at night when I was thinking about why Mom forgot to pick me up at school. Why she always monopolized my friends. Why I was the butt of her jokes. You never stopped by while I wrote my stories. I guess you were writing your poems.

To My Atheist

>   I do not believe in the God
>   you do not believe in
>   either

Uncle Morty, I would not dare
argue against your adamant atheism
now that you are dead.

It isn't fair, you can just cross your arms
and smile and say NO.
No, I can't prove anything.
No, there is no reason to pray, to mourn,
to have a ceremony, to think
you might hear a word I am saying
or that you will sit back or lie back I guess,
and say *oh, now I understand. You were right, Ray.
Here I am up here, or down here and I hear
what you are saying. Thank you!*

No, I would not argue that you hear
one damned word of what I am saying,
but I will tell you this anyway.

Yesterday
the people who loved you
for what you were and what you did,
whatever you happened to believe or didn't,
the people who would like to continue to love you
got together and propped each other up
and laughed and cried
and told stories and this was God.

They talked about what was good in you
and found it in themselves, so they resolved
to be more like the good you and less like the bad you
and this was God. And it was God when your daughter
looked like you and talked like you
only I don't mean
to insult your intelligence.

Of course there is no God and you can't hear
a word, a damned word I am saying,
but I'm saying it anyway because I want to tell you
I would like to go on loving you
even though there is no reason,
none whatsoever, to do so now that you are gone.
But I do. And guess what that is.

The Fuller Brush Man Doesn't Stop Here Anymore

Black leather case in hand,
full of gadgetry no house
or housewife should be without.
He wore a bow tie, the first one I ever saw in real life,
a pocket square and lots of teeth.
My mother shooed him away with a curt
"No, I don't need anything,"
and closed the door to her house.
I felt sorry for him walking in the Miami sun.

Now here he is, coming up the long walk.
The heavy case seems so light
He swings it slightly.
Up the steps.
Is he whistling?
No, he's humming a tune I think I know.
The bell tolls throughout the house. No way to avoid it.
I open the door. He is tall and no matter how old
or big I am, he would be taller.

He comes in with a nod, a pleasant grin.
He's done this before.
He isn't working, he knows we want
what he's selling. We need what he's got.
He goes to my father's big chair,
sits comfortably, clicks the lock with a graceful sweep
of his long, pale thumb
and and opens the bag.

Perfectly ordered, perfectly placed.
He has what we want.
Candy-colored handles over
white, white bristles.
Clean enough to scrub
everything
clean as new.

He pushes the case toward me.
I lean forward beneath his knowing smile.

An Epiphany

I want to live in the future where there is a cure for everything
I want to live in the future where poor people live like rich people do today
I want to live in the future where computers actually work
and when people watch Star Trek they say
What? didn't they have that back then?
Where there is a ten- hour work week but it's OK
because there are 6,000 tv/internet channels implanted
in our heads

I want to live in the future where poets are paid like athletes
and loved like rock stars.
Well, maybe not

I want to live in the future where people's minds live
as long as their bodies and bodies work
as long as people live
I want to live in the future where sex is safe again
the future where it is safe to be a child
the future where science and religion are not in conflict
the future where getting there is not
the most expensive part of travel or education
the future where the future is now
and now is then
is history
is the good old days
no matter how bad they may actually be
no matter how they should make me
dread the future that will be

Portrait of the Artist

Annabel Person was famous for her coloring-book style art. Distinct black shapes partially filled-in with Burnt Sienna, Blue Violet, Shamrock and other Crayola colors. A pack of crayons were attached to the frame, inviting the viewer into the seemingly uncompleted work. Her Stupid Dreams series included square-jawed husbands, beatific children, smiling women and titles like Lies, Lies and Trapped by Talent. She lived very alone. The morning she was found on the sidewalk ten floors beneath her balcony, her landlord took note of her unfinished self-portrait, a half-empty bottle of expensive chardonnay and an open Care Bears coloring book, its pages yellowed and dog-eared. Someone had colored outside the lines. The police cordoned off the area with Laser Lemon tape, moved her body to the morgue and drew a chalk outline where she lay.

Would the word innocence ever come up? Would you know what that is? Would you still want to hear that this is all a story meaning something else and all in my mind, me overreacting to having a somewhat difficult childhood and not to any form of abuse? Would you say that the truth lies somewhere between the extremes? Doesn't it always?

Would it matter if I said I was molested or abused or used? If I was screwed or got fucked? If I was screwer or screwee? Does it matter when you are talking about a child?

I got fucked and it was bad and it was good. Isn't it always? You might ask how I can be so funny and write such charming poems and make amusing observations. How else could I survive?

You might ask whether I believe in God. Where was God? How could God allow this to happen to a child? I don't blame God. I believe in God, although maybe not your God. How could God let this happen? How could you? Yes, I believe in God. Because I have seen what happens when He is not in the room.

I want to explain myself. I want to find a way to do it that will make you understand. I will show you a movie. It is one of the movies I made up while I was trying not to be where I was.

Here is my movie:

The old man stirred the black pot slowly as the steam rose and a tempting fragrance filled the air. He turned down the heat on the electric stove. The boy sat very still. He did not know what to do with his hands.

Did you learn anything, boy? Did you see how it was? I threw the lifting spell at the objects on the table and what happened?

The boy looked at the table. The objects were sitting as still as he was trying to sit. A small tree branch, a lump of iron, a small, thick steel plate, a plastic fork. Not sixty seconds earlier all were in the air, hovering above the table. All but the plastic fork which was standing on its tines with its handle in the air, wavering. The steel plate was highest, then the iron, then the wood, which was just above the fork.

The boy looked down and then at the table again. He started to repeat what he said and caught himself just as he exhaled the first word. He swallowed and said

What happened was your spell affected the steel most, the iron, next most the wood less than the iron. And it only slightly moved the plastic fork.

Did a smile flicker at the edges of the old man's lips? He turned to the pot, stirred it and turned down the heat another notch. He put the lid on the pot and turned suddenly.

Well?

The boy pursed his lips and then leaned forward. He swallowed again and then spoke in a steady voice.

It doesn't seem to make any sense because logic, I mean science… He swallowed and shook his head once. *Excuse me. I mean* popular *science says that the fork is lightest and the steel heaviest. Maybe the iron but the steel plate is bigger so it should be heavier but it wasn't.*

Again he stopped and shook his head once. He closed his eyes and then opened them and looked squarely at the old man.

Not heavier. What I mean is your spell should have had greater effect on the plastic fork than the steel and so on because it was acting against the weight, the physical weight of the four things. The steel IS heavier in weight, in physical weight…no, in weight as measured by popular science. But the spell worked more on it than the other things…objects…because it was the true *science.*

So what I saw was that the physical weight of an object does not affect its resistance to the strength of the spell. That is what you were showing me.

The old man smiled slightly.

Very good, he nodded. *And wrong*

A Dream Story

And when there lifted from The City the darkness that some said was night and others insisted something more, there was a great rejoicing until the people heard the wailing of mothers and saw that the first of the sacred children had been carried off. And so for all the nights that followed, the mothers slept with their arms around their children and the fathers sat keeping vigil and yet in the morning one or another of the children, the sacred and blessed children that were the only hope and salvation of the people of The City, disappeared in the instant the father coughed or the mother placed her hand on the bed to steady herself as she rose. Disappeared without a cry or a call for help. Disappeared into the morning sun as it flared over the distant mountains. Then the people of The City cried to the four kings and the six priests and all the wise men and all the warrior chieftans. Then, no longer willing to trust the kings or the priests or the warlords to act in their behalf, they prayed to the gods themselves, the great gods of fire, air and water and the lesser gods of joy and song, even to the dark gods whose names a few dared utter, so desperate was their need. But no one, not the kings or the gods or the men wise or powerful, were able to return the children to The City. The people tried to protect their children and prayed, waited, grew old, died and were forgotten. But the children were not gone at all, and although they called to their parents and begged the gods to let them be heard, they were unable to do anything but watch and grow older, marry and have children of their own. All this within the walls of The City where they live and love one another and mourn the parents who sleep in their same beds and await the darkness that may be something great and terrible or simply the natural turning and returning of the earth as it must and always will.

Titanic Dream

What if instead of musicians playing "Nearer My God To Thee" a comedian was the onboard entertainer standing on the deck of the Titanic, continuing his patter as the ship listed, groaned and sank, having decided that, facing certain death anyway, he would go out doing what he was born to do, his God-given talent for doing impressions of Queen Victoria, the Kaiser, whoever, and asking the people frantically rushing to the overfilled lifeboats where they were from?

What Death Is This?

Let me get right to the point:
Death is not a scythe-wielding,
humorless Swede in a cowled robe.
No, and he is not a sweet-faced old man
with a twinkle in his eye and a faint
Irish accent, or a beautiful woman in
a long flowing white robe.

He is not an owl waiting
to carry us off to a river of light,
although I like that one.

Or a tiny virus with a bad attitude,
or an unfriendly giant, or a friendly giant,
or wind or ice or night
or anything like these.

I've seen the young and beautiful
taken and lost to me
while the old and awful
and people in pain
linger on. There is only one way
to make sense of it all:

I am convinced
that Death is a cartoon,
a garishly attired pink-faced
goober with big ears
or, I don't know, maybe
a cartoon animal,
a purple possum
or a red cockroach,
with a voice
like Archie Bunker or Mae West
or like the President.

Wouldn't that be a trip?
Can you imagine yourself
as the sparking dynamite rolls your way,

and the comic sledgehammer
socks you in the kisser
and the Acme Anvil Co. anvil
falls on your head
so you crash through the floor
leaving a hole in the shape of your
body

and you fall and fall,
still laughing your fool head off,
while the camera focuses
on Death's delighted
Porky Pig face.

as it stutters a goodbye
and that dreadful,
infectious, grotesque
song plays and replays
so loud, so merry,
that it cannot be real.

Fordham Evers Kidnapped A Busload Of Tourists On Their Way To The Top Of Mount Early

He directed the driver, Ralph Smathers, to take a seat in the sixth row. Mr. Evers took the wheel and was silent as he drove up the winding road. Mr. Smathers was heard by those in the fifth and seventh rows, with the exception of Elizabeth Tompkins who was too deaf to hear and some whispered too vain to admit it, to mutter that Evers was taking them on the same route they were following in the first place.

There was cell service most most of the way and eleven calls were made to 911. Mt. Early is one of the highest peaks in this part of the Carolinas. The crest has been partially cleared, yielding a scenic vista to the south and east that includes the steeples of the four churches in Graysville, a town of two thousand or more in season and less than one-third that the rest of the year.

The bus broke down just after Mr. Evers turned off the main road onto a dirt and gravel trail, hardly a road at all, marked only by a solitary and ancient mailbox bearing the name "Evers". Mr. Evers climbed down and looked at the engine. He then walked back to invite the bus riders to step out, which only a few did as it was cool at that elevation and the roadside was thick with undergrowth.

They were all standing about, some angry and most afraid, when I drove up. I saw the bus standing a few yards off the main road, blocking the way up the mountain. I put on my lights and gave the siren a pulse. Mr. Evers walked toward the patrol car slowly. He betrayed no emotion. His revolver remained tucked in his belt.

I trained my Glock on him and ordered him to place his hands on his head and kneel down. He complied with no protest or discernible expression. After I cuffed his bony hands I took the weapon. I saw that it was empty.

"What the blue blazes did you think you were you doing, Mr. Evers?" I asked. He was well known in Graysville, a tall, quiet recluse who rarely came down the mountain, never during tourist season.

"I needed to show someone" was all he said, turning his head around to me. That, and then, "I needed 'em to see."

It was something in his good eye, the left one, that stopped me from putting him in the cruiser. I turned him around.

"What?"

He did not answer, but continued to stare at me. It occurred to me that I should know what he wanted, but I did not. I don't know why I uncuffed him and followed as he walked past the bus, but I did.

"Where the hell are you going?" Mr. Smathers asked. I confirmed that no one was hurt and the sirens coming up the mountain assured me they wouldn't have long to wait.

We were a few steps up the trail when Mr. Evers answered the question in my mind.

"About two miles."

The path narrowed as it wound up the mountain and became steep. I wondered if Mr. Evers thought the tourists would be able to walk past the point where it was overgrown with rhododendron on one side and a moss-covered rock face on the other. He stopped, leaned against an oak and held his side. Behind him, maybe a hundred yards back, a ghost-grey chestnut still stood like a chimney, its branches long gone and its top broken off.

"Are you ill, Mr. Evers?"

"Yes," was all he said as he continued on. It was not a very hard climb but I was winded and sweating when the trail ended at a level clearing.

The entire grounds were green, so bright after the dark, tree-canopied path that it hurt my eyes. A little stream ran along one side and splashed noisily as it flowed over smooth, glistening rocks. At the other end, and a few yards past the stream, the forest formed a dark boundary around the cleared space.

In the middle sat the house. Log cabins, outside Hollywood and children's imaginations, are rough and uneven. The logs rarely fit well. (Of course, I am ignoring the obscene pre-fabricated dollhouses advertised as summer homes). This one was perfect. The wood was dark and smooth with age. A path of carefully-selected flat stones led to the door and the flower box beneath each window was bright with color.

On one side of the cabin was a well-tended garden and beyond it the Smokies spread row-on-row until they faded into the sky. I must have gasped at the sight because Mr. Evers turned and his dour expression seemed to flicker a smile for an instant. We walked up the path into the open doorway,

The house was sunny, large windows at the rear covering most of the wall and running from two feet below the high ceiling nearly to the floor. Only snowbirds and those who design and build for them put glass on the rear of houses, where the summer heat and winter cold enter at will. I have lived in Gray County all my life. The view from the Evers place was exceptional. I did not fault Mr. Evers for inviting it into his home.

An enormous, scrupulously clean fireplace of native rock occupied most of one wall. On the other were paintings of local scenes I recognized, including the Evers property and its vista. I noticed the initials "L. E".

There was a small, round dining table with two chairs. A pottery vase, hand-thrown, was in the center, filled with long-stemmed flowers. As I walked to the windows I saw that behind the house, overlooking the view, were two hand-carved tombstones. A newly-cut bunch of wildflowers was placed beneath the one reading "Lil." The earth was bare beneath the one reading "Ford."

That was when I turned to see Mr. Evers seated in a handmade rocking chair, his eyes fixed on the window and the trace of a smile on his lips. Neither the chair nor his chest was moving in the gentle afternoon sunlight that flooded his room and chased its shadows into the night.

Let me take a deep breath. And back up a bit.

When I was very young I was raped by a friend of my mother's.
You might call it a seduction but that would be too kind. She took advantage. At first I really didn't understand and after that she used shame to make me do it and then I began to want it because it felt good and doing it meant I was an adult.
Don't we all want to be adults?
Even now.

And the day came when I no longer needed to be your daughter. When I no longer needed candy at Valentine's Day or a silly teddy bear for my birthday. I just wish you'd told me about it before you decided that day had come.

When I no longer needed to be your daughter was when I should have had the opportunity to want to be.

Little Match Girl

who the hell wrote this story who the hell wrote about
a poor little girl who freezes to death selling
matches so her father will not beat her and why the hell
did someone tell me the story but with a happy ending
and then my mother had to tell me in strictest confidence
that the little match girl freezes to death in a doorway
what kind of story is that to tell a little boy
what kind of mother feels compelled to tell a child
the truth and what is so bloody Christian about Hans
Anderson if he tells this damned story?

I always saw Shirley Temple as the match girl my mother
grew up thinking she was Shirley Temple and my sister
thought she was Shirley Temple and I hated Shirley Temple
and her movies that were on Saturday afternoons when
there were wars to fight on the other channels
and ships to sink and Fokkers to shoot down and even long
slow baseball games with Dizzy Dean and Pee Wee Reese
and the Red Sox always lost to the Yankees but that was better
than Shirley Temple Mickey Mantle was better than Shirley
Temple I thought and I wanted Shirley Temple
to freeze to death in a doorway and take my sister with her

and then Shirley Temple became Shirley Temple Black
who did all those nice things for children all over the world
and made sure there were no little match girls in
Uganda Peru Cambodia Bangladesh and places where
I had to eat my vegetables or the children would starve
only my mother said it was Europe where no more
people starved than in Arizona but what did she know
she is the one who said the poor little match girl froze
in a doorway and we lived in Miami so who knew from
freezing and that bit someone who wasn't my mother
told me about her grandmother taking her to heaven
I could never buy that because dead is dead like my sister's
turtle (who may have only been sleeping but certainly died
when we buried him) besides we were and are Jewish and all that
Christian Anderson Dutch Aryan blond heaven stuff didn't
play for me because I believe in the here and now
and Shirley Temple did nothing for me singing in her starchy
dress white socks patent leather shoes patented cute curls
and dimples but Shirley Temple Black was really pretty cool
and a helluva better person than Hans Christian
Bloody Mouthed Anderson or Mickey Mantle
who beat up on the Red Sox and drank and whored himself to death
or my sister and her dead turtle or my mother for that matter
and yes I am sorry I just said that

You might ask where my parents were and didn't I act strangely or didn't my grades go down? No, my grades were fine but I did lose respect for my parents because now I was a man. Isn't being an adult all about having sex, as much sex as you want? I did. I didn't care about my friends and I knew my parents couldn't protect me but I didn't need protection anyway because now I could make love to a woman standing up or from behind and I could last for an hour and I doubted even my father could do it as well as I could and I knew this because this woman wanted me and not him.

And then she brought another woman so I was really a man. I could have sex with two women at once and I was still young, I won't tell you how young but I was old enough to do it and I could do it again and again and I was good at it, really good and then, this other woman I will call this other woman Mrs. Jones, Mrs. Jones one day brought her husband.

And I did not like it but some of it was ok and all that mattered was that I could do it and so I did. A lot.

My movie continues:

Wrong but a good answer. Very good, actually.

The boy did not smile. He looked down and then back at the old man.

Why? I mean what was happening, what should I have learned?

Oh, you did learn. And exactly what you should. And you have shown me that you are ready to learn more.

Here, my boy, it is very simple, and very hard for most people to even begin to grasp.

You know that weight is merely a function of gravity. As Einstein showed, gravity is the most important force in the universe. Oh, he didn't say it that way but if he had only lived a few more centuries he would have come to understand it, I am sure.

Gravity bends time and light and in fact it is the single most potent… anything… there is. Period. But gravity does not act only on what popular science calls mass. Mass is in fact a much more complex concept.

The steel was weakest against the spell, even though it would weigh the most on any scale and would be hardest for a normal person to break with any tool. The iron was actually heavier as it was a natural substance, pulled from the earth in a raw state, whereas the steel was fabricated by man. The iron in the steel was forced to give up its self and the result was a slave to the will of the steelmaker.

You take it further now. What about the wood?

The boy started to stand and, seeing a sudden scowl on the old man's face sat back down and spoke slowly.

The wood is natural, too. But the wood was alive. It was torn from the tree…no, that twig fell off last night, didn't it. If it had been torn it would be weaker…lighter.

The boy spoke faster, his eyes wide and his mouth smiling.

The steel had the least mass, the least importance? no…yes, that is what I mean, importance, because it was iron turned into something else and then the wood because it was natural and also alive, or formerly alive. If you had cut it from the tree it would be less heavy because you had already imposed your will on it.

I will interrupt to help you over the next roadblock…there are many other factors that would determine whether a twig cut from a tree has more or less…importance is very, very good indeed…importance or selfhood is the way I might say it….than the iron but always more than the unformed piece of steel. Now, what about the fork?

Hello again.
Are you having a good time reading my story?
Are you uncomfortable with me or bored with the story of the magic stuff?
Who the hell are you?

You are the hell and I was in the hell and where were you, Mommy? Where were you, Father? I will tell you where they were while I was in hell and they were not. They did notice that something was wrong, of course, because I was doing the worst thing a child can do. I was not torturing animals or killing other children or setting fires or stealing. No, I was doing far worse. I was disobedient. I was disrespectful. But I was too old for spanking and too young to take away car keys or ground me. They didn't ground kids in those days because kids had not yet learned to fly all over the place like they do today. So they did the only thing they could. They took me to a psychiatrist.

They took me to Dr. Jones.

Who was Mrs. Jones's husband. That's right. THAT Mrs. Jones. He had an office in his home, wasn't that convenient?

But wait. There's more.

I Saw Death In Your Backseat

I saw Death in your backseat
as you left the parking lot.
I called to you, waived my arms,
ran behind the car and then
drove after you.

I almost caught up at the second light
and there was Death,
looking out the rear windshield,
smiling at me.
He flashed me the peace sign,
or was it V for Victory?

At the next light he winked
and gave me the finger as you drove on.
It was like that urban myth
about the woman being chased
down a lonely country road
by a guy flashing his lights.

I flashed my lights.
I honked the horn once.
Twice.
You finally pulled over
and I ran to you.
Your backseat was empty.
You really don't want me to go,
you laughed, *Do you?*

First, more of my story:

The boy sat and thought. The old man removed the pot from the stove and set it aside. He cleaned the kitchen and removed a loaf of bread from the oven…

Sir?

Ah. Ready?

You once told me that things exist to serve. We were at the jeweler's and you pointed to a diamond ring in one case and a cheap watch on the counter and asked which was worth more. I think you said which was 'more'. You told me the watch was more than the diamond.

That didn't seem to make sense then and it doesn't now because the watch was made by people and the ring was mostly a natural stone. But I think you were saying that the watch DOES something and the ring just sits there.

(The old man nodded slowly, his face blank.)

Let me help you again. You are very close.

The piece of steel was cut off a plate shipped from a steel fabrication company. The rest of the plate was used to make a machine used to make automobile parts. Some sort of stamping device on a conveyer belt at a factory, I think.

Now, if we had a piece of machine, it would have been much…heavier…because it was part of a working, moving unit. A machine that did *something. It would take a very powerful spell to move such a machine or even a piece of it. The raw steel, on the other hand, was merely a man-made substance without form or purpose.*

The plastic fork had much more true mass than the shard of steel. Even though it was also man-made, it already has a purpose. It cannot make something else, it doesn't really *do* anything except assist a hand in moving food to the mouth"

The old man paused and raised his eyebrows. He smiled and waited. The boy thought a moment and then spoke.

You are saying that, as important as being natural or alive is in determining…self? mass, power… it is more *important that a thing can do something and is meant to do something. The watch kept time…I mean it showed time, which is important to the people who made it.*

The old man walked to the boy and put his hand on the boy's shoulder.

Good. And if the watch did more, if it had a light built in to show the way in the dark, if it played music or especially if it could be used to make music, it would have even more power, more self, more importance, more true mass because it could not only show it could, in a sense create.

The boy turned and spoke quickly, *But what about people? Living things? Animals or plants?*

Ah, at last. That, my boy, is what I might call the true mass of today's lesson and of everything you have learned so far.

The old man paused and leaned into his pupil.

All living things are engines, they are burning fires. The fuel for that fire is the thing's true mass. What we do, what we are, builds our true mass. My studies work for me, they feed me, because they are me. For some it is a walk in the country. For a plant, it may be its flower. For an animal each escape from a predator.

Relationships with others may strengthen or deplete us. Everyone knows that, The sorcerer winked, *They just don't know why.*

There is much, much more, but that is enough for today. Wash your hands, set the table and let's have some of this soup.

And that is how it was until I went to college.
But I got good reviews from my doctor. Who also coached me in how to act and not be myself which simply means he was a teacher. Isn't that what teachers do? He taught me and coached me and I learned to cope like that serial killer on tv who learned to kill only bad people. I learned how to act and how not to be myself. Dr. Jones, he taught me a lot of other things.

> The night I really grew up was not the night I became an adult. It was the night I became aware of the world, the night I realized there was something wrong in the world. It was the night the world changed, not me. That night, I came home and you were still up. You were in your den as always. I kissed you goodnight. You didn't notice the liquor on my breath or that I wasn't wearing my bra. I told myself it was because I was only fourteen.

**My Wife Marvels At My Hunting Knife
Before the Brownie Camping Trip**

She asks a silly question..
Of course we kill.
We are born with death in our hearts.

When the Angel taps our lips
we remember only
that we will die,
our engineered obsolescence
like plastic parts in a Lincoln.
We are born with death in our hearts.

What else does she expect
when she delights in the design
of this survival knife?
Lethal blade,
built-in compass,
saw teeth,
fire-starter,
survival
knife.

Don't tell me you fantasize about
roasting s'mores
or leading the pack from the woods.

L_____ can't sleep.
She hears something ticking.
Hush now, and close your eyes, my sweet girl.

It's just Peter Pan's crocodile
shadowing Captain Hook across your dreams.
Tomorrow we'll pitch a tent in the garden.
I'll be here when you wake.
I love you to death.

"As Hell"

it's loud as Hell out there
        yes this makes sense
        Hell would be loud
        not presence of sound
        (screams sobs
         mechanical grinding)
        but absence of quietude

it's cold as Hell today
        viz Dante
        absence of warmth
        and all its associations

lonely as Hell
        got it
        been there
hot as Hell
        obvious
dark as Hell
        maybe…
        absence of light
        of vision
        of knowing where the Hell I am
        what's ahead
        who's out there

scary as Hell
        yup
pretty as Hell
        nope
good as Hell
        just plain wrong

fast as Hell
          huh?
funny as Hell
          not for me
          you?

hard as Hell
          ah!
          as in Sisyphus
          yes
          been there
          again and

mad as Hell
          me too

bad as Hell
painful as Hell
mean as Hell
          all good
          or bad

old as Hell
          don't get it
          not yet no
          not yet

Doc Holliday Says Goodbye to Wyatt Earp
-Glenwood Springs, Colorado, 1887

What do you want me to tell you? Should I say Tom and Frank McLaury stopped by last night to say things were really ace-high down there in hell because they could boil potatoes in the creeks and light their stogies on the nearest rock? Or an angel who looked like Big Nose Kate drifted down through the ceiling, wrapped her wings around my thighs and hummed Nearer My God to Thee as her halo kept bumping against my navel?

You figure that one out, Alterboy.

Maybe you want to me to smile like a saint and tell you I hear a heavenly choir every time I cough up a bloody bit of my lungs

No, Compadre, that would be a lie as bad as saying I came out here because Sherman burned Georgia or because they said it was good for my health to breathe dust and horseshit and kill every man who looked at me without a sense of irony.

I love irony, in fact I find this whole damned thing funny.

Well, I did head west because of my lungs but I stayed because here I could get closer to why I was dealt a losing hand. Isn't it ironic that I was able to kill because I didn't care if I died? My hand never wavered, I never drew too soon or fretted whether some drunk cowboy might have a brother, death having this way of freeing your mind, of making things clear and simple. I just coughed up what I didn't need along with my lungs. I coughed up my conscience. I coughed up my home and then my family and then social conventions like not killing some fool who spit tobacco on my boots and then I coughed up and spat out friends, except you and you were supposed to die like your brother Morgan, only you didn't, damn your black eyes, you didn't catch a cold while everyone from sweet old Fred White to Curly Bill got shot and crippled or killed. Well, God bless you, Wyatt. I mean that. Poor old Johnny Ringo got shot and it is a damned shame whoever did it shot him in the side of that pretty face Kate seemed to like so much and propped his body against that tree. God bless him too.

At this point God may as well bless everyone, I really don't care, but I do want it known that I never once wept over my luck or blamed anyone else for any of this life. Every time I drew a gun or a dead man's hand I just shook my head and coughed and had a drink and coughed some more like there was something I needed to get off my chest but there wasn't and there isn't so don't be thinking otherwise. I am just trying getting used to being in something the size of this bed for a long damned time.

So here's the valediction: you go to Alaska or New York or Paris or somewhere and you write a dime novel about your life or find some other way to tell the lies.

You have a good long oxygen-soaked life but you just tell anyone who asks that John Henry Holliday never drew to an inside straight, never shot a man in the back who didn't have it coming, and died thanking the Almighty for a good ride. It's been a good life and a good time and a worthwhile exercise and, like any properly- adjusted hog's leg, my aim is dead on what's in front of me. I thank God for my blessings and blame myself for everything else.

Komodo

the giant monitor lizard lives only on the island of Komodo
it is the largest lizard it eats every living thing and any dead thing
it can find its mouth is full of teeth and deadly bacteria
it is an ambush predator
I saw it on tv lying in ambush for a water buffalo a water buffalo
dangerous and powerful and able to outrun a Komodo monitor lizard
but from ambush the lizard bit the buffalo on its leg the buffalo's leg I mean
and the buffalo ran bleeding and the lizard just walked after it
for days it walked after it after it had bit it and could track its smell
because the lizard smells with its tongue and soon it was infected
the buffalo's leg I mean and for days the buffalo walked around
the island of Komodo festering its leg I mean dying the buffalo I mean
and soon other monitor lizards smelled with their tongues the infection
and at a water hole the buffaloes were drinking and all ran
except the bit one who was so sick of it the bite I mean
the infection the sickness the pain the lameness the poison in its blood
that it the buffalo just stood and then sort of sat and it the lizard
and they the other lizards bit off huge jagged chunks of it and ate it alive its eye
its eye it the buffalo made no sound after a while but the one eye
facing the camera and so me that eye I mean was wild with fear and pain
and nature this is nature isn't it
and I know you'd rather hear about bunnies
and swans that are not ducklings and maybe meerkats that eat bugs
but this is the nature I know
and the buffalo know and the lizards the Komodo monitor lizards
that you virgins are so afraid of
because you think the world the natural world
should be what it should be and not what it is
and you are afraid you virgins of the fact
that the monitor lizard is called dragon

And there was this one thing through all of it, all the women. And men. Who fucked me and I fucked them.

Through all of it I kept wondering. Well, not at first but after a while I kept wondering what it was that I was supposed to feel. Why was this wrong and secret? I remembered that I did not like it and it scared and hurt me at first and for a while after but why did people only fuck one other person and get married so they could only fuck one other person and even that fucking word fuck I knew it was the right word but

> I went with Tommy Lee that night because he liked me. He told me so. He told me there would be a party. I went for the pot and the beer. What I didn't know I was that I was the party. I went because he said he liked me. That explained everything. So you never had to.

it was such a small word and this was so much more and a lot more fun and, of course, I liked some of the women and maybe one of the men. Not Dr. Jones. But no one like the redheaded lady. I thought there was something special about when I was with the redheaded lady with the very white skin. She was Vanessa and that is her name because it is so pretty I want to use it. I will not tell you her last name or say anything bad about her because every time I, you know, came inside her I was so very happy.

But I still thought I would explode. I began writing poetry. Poetry I showed no one. Except I read one to Vanessa. She smiled at me and said the worst thing anyone can say. "That's nice," she said. As she took off her bra. She said my poem was nice.

is it still a poem if you write it when you are having a nervous breakdown * is it still a poem if you don't really mean it * is it still true if it is a poem * or if you don't really mean it * is it still a poem if you write it every day * is it still the truth if you discover it when you are having a nervous breakdown * is it still a nervous breakdown * if it happens every day

And then I went to college. And then my mother died of breast cancer. And then I met this one girl in college. Betty was her name.

And then everything changed.

I made love to Betty and it was like Vanessa. But not like Vanessa. I never saw Vanessa again. Or Dr. Jones or Mrs. Jones.

You would like to hear that I learned what love is and it superseded sex, nasty sex. You would like to hear that Betty and I lived happily ever after. Or maybe you would like to hear that I killed her, the bitch. Shame on you. I loved her after that first time I really made love. I convinced myself we had something in common. I believed that with her I would not be alone. But there was neither happily ever after nor murder. Too bad. Either one would make a good story. Neither would be true.

Your Body Your Body

your body
I think about your body
how perfect it is for me how I want
to hold your body and how it
wants me pulls me in
takes me and gives me so much
your body so
                                        sweet
your body that you own
but you share with me its privacy
with me your body
but why is it that
I think so much about
                your body
                  my darling
when it is your mind
I fell in love with

I didn't make a big deal about not talking to you. You were always busy. Occupied is a better word. You were always occupied. I thought it might be because you wanted a son. Maybe that is why I am who I am. Maybe it was that night with Tommy Lee. Maybe I was born this way. I really don't care. I am fine with it. Your stories about unicorns and dragons and later spirits and spacemen did not only make me a writer. They made me able to live with unlimited possibilities.

Flying In Bed On Sunday Morning

To wake alone again,
to wake alone.
To the mirror-on-mirror of another day,
each breath a hurricane in the still air
above the half-empty bed.

  I was the world in which I walked

I cannot rise,
not yet,
to be blown about by
the hours I keep in tenths,
the world I would watch
from a safe distance.

  to speak of worlds, and to live in them

I am more.
I am not merely
these thoughts,
words scattered on a page,
wind harnessed briefly to make sound,
dust molded into man for a moment,
I am more than motes and croaks blown
before a wind I cannot name.

No matter what I read I hear
Valery:
  The wind is rising…we must try to live
Kumin:
  We gather speed for the last run
  And lift off into the weather.

It has been so long
since I walked outside,
since I shuddered against the wind.
I am shuttered against the wind.

  each year is harder to live within
  each year is harder to live without

The years behind mock the years ahead.
I would make more of my time.
I would demand the world live for me.
I would insist on joy.
I would pick up the phone.

   - O remember
   In your narrowing hours
   That more things move
   Than blood in the heart

I want more than this,
though it means stepping off
a bed,
a cliff,
only the air to sustain my steps

that I may attempt to live in a world
where each day begins
forgetting the night's dreams
and then like any bold pilot
putting down the flight plan
and trusting the naked air.

Quotations are from The Open Door: 100 Poems, 100 Years of Poetry Magazine, poems by W. Stevens, p.63, R. Creeley, p. 62, C. Arnold, p. 57 and L. Bogan, p.70

This is a true story.
Betty and I were married and we had a little girl and my life could have been perfect.

I know because I watched it like I was reading a novel that was a true story just like the Bible is a true story. I believe that and I am not being sacrilegious. I am very sorry if you think I am but I am not being sacrilegious to God or the bible or to what happened to me. This is the truth. The Bible is not merely a tale of what happened.

We do not know all that is true and what we know is true is not all of it.

and Abraham felt the chill of the desert air as he looked at the stars shivering in the blackness and he heard the first wail of his son the son who would carry his name and his blood and his seed and by this give his soul eternal life and he ran to the tent and took the boy child and walked outside where his god could see him and he raised Issac to the sky and the child the boy child the son who was Isaac was Abraham was forever Isaac cried and the cry was LIFE LIFE LIFE and in that moment Abraham knew that he would die and Isaac would die and forever would die and that he must kill this boy because he Abraham was not important he did not matter his petty desire to live did not matter the boy was life the boy was God and in the face of God Abraham knew he was nothing and did not matter * nor did his bargain * and that is what happened at the foot of Mt. Moriah, * ah, children * that is what really happened * only a parent can understand * and God

That's how I felt until things went bad in ways I did not think they could.

I Woke With A Dream Of Your Father

he was hauling fresh produce from Andalusia to Atlanta the way you told me he did all those years for some reason he was in a moving van instead of his farm truck he was trying to conserve fuel it wastes fuel to brake the way you told me it does his van was straining to get up steep hills it was hurtling down steep hills for some reason this was in Montana maybe Carolina the van was making that horrible gear grate engine bellow he was barely in control the weight threatening to hurl him off the mountain it was for some reason the Rockies I think it might have been the Smokies at the turn ahead of him there was a low rock wall there were tourists taking photos he was heading for them down the steepest hill where the road takes a sharp left turn where they are standing it was your father who can barely walk often forgets his grandaughter's name your father his hands on the wheel his eyes wide in the dream and in the dream I am writing this in a poem a poem about your father the van the hills the horrible noise because in the dream I can make sense of it all.

Fred Didn't Want to Have Sex

Fred didn't want to have sex
      so Shirley said he was cold.
He didn't want to go to the beach
      so she said he was a stick-in-the-mud.
He didn't tell her that he loved her
(or if he did she didn't remember)
      so she said he was traited for Aspergers.

Fred didn't want to have sex
      so Shirley said he was gay,
      maybe latently,
      but still.
And because he didn't like her chicken divan,
      Julia Roberts movies or the wallpaper,
      he had no taste.

Fred still didn't want to have sex
      so Shirley said he was a sadistic bastard
      and since he still wouldn't go to the beach
      or a Julia Roberts movie or tell her
      that he loved her when he knew
      perfectly well that he did,
      he was just plain stubborn.

And damned lucky to have her.

Dear Betty:

the truth is * when I touch you I feel better * until I remember it is me who is touching you * the truth is I want to protect you * not from who I am * I want to protect you * because of who I am not able to be

Ray

I found that note one morning when I woke up with an empty bottle of King George V on the floor and a mirror and credit card and half of a drinking straw on the nightstand:

> To whom it may concern:
>
> what to do
> what to do with this life this one life this one life you are blessed with this one life it is one life it is your only life this life what to do with this your only life
>
> what if it was not one life only but more more lives more life to live
>
> what if
> what if you could trade a few hours at the back end for someone's beautiful singing voice and then being a good trader a smart shopper you traded a few more hours to a dying genius and were now smarter so smart what if you used those smarts to convince a handsome man who was in danger to trade his face and an autistic man his ability to calculate long streams of numbers I bet he would just give that up and a suicidal woman would trade the last years of the life she didn't want for a moment's peace and so on
>
> what if you could
> what if you could trade for memories for love for so much life that you lived more more lives a thousand lives all perfect beautiful wonderful lives yours all yours what if you could
>
> would that help
> would you do more with a more perfect life or a longer life ten lives stacked like calendar pages would you do more then Mr. Sweet Singing Genius would you do more be more see more more than you do one night holding one person one other life that you make better you dumb fuck you dumb fuck it is not about your life your one life or one hundred lives it is not about that it is not about you or your one life it is about this
>
> it is about that you will be * until you are not needed * and then you will not be no more never again
>
> Sincerely, Raymond Shaw

Depression

As the god hopped from mountaintop to mountaintop, it perceived the cold and the wetness of the snow but felt neither, of course. Feeling is reserved for humans and animals. The god, although not really a god, could only perceive such things intellectually, processing the feelings he observed so closely that it was almost like experiencing them. That was one reason it chose to remain on earth and walked among the living often.

The god sat on the top of the highest mountain and observed snow being blown from peaks about it. Its eyes were not like human eyes, not like the eyes of any earthbound beast. It saw objects in a cubist fashion, from many perspectives at once. This made the beauty of the scene all the more vibrant than anything capable of feelings. The god knew this and for an instant fooled itself into believing that it was anything but curious. It saw the dawn paint the eastern sky a thin line of near-purple pink and watched as the glow became redder and was reflected in the ice atop the mountains.

The god sighed. A certain near-sadness, an emptiness that was very close to melancholy, swept over it. Again it envied humans. The simplicity of their design, the innocence of their minds. They believed the physiology of the dinosaur, the forces of physics, the sunrise and the tardigrade to be evidence of a Divine plan. Yet they were capable, in some primitive way, of appreciating the intense beauty of this world as the god could not.

Once, while posing as a beggar in an ancient city, the god allowed the populous to observe a tiny fraction of its power. It saved a child by drawing it up from a well with a wave of its hand. Why it did so is hard to explain. Most likely, it was trying to awaken some sensation, some emotion like those it saw in the frantic humans.

For its trouble, it experienced only a deeper curiosity and the same flat emptiness it had always known. No joy, no pride, no warm feelings of paternalism.

It was assaulted by absurd praise and the worship of all about, who proclaimed it a god and offered it sacrifice (someone even proposed sacrificing the child). The god experienced this for a moment and found it, too, unsatisfying. It flashed away, leaving only a smell of incense and temporary blindness on all who were staring at it.

How long ago was that? The god shook its head. It looked into the sky. Its vision telescoped beyond the atmosphere, past the moon and edges of the solar system and beyond until it found a comet speeding its way toward a distant star. The god considered for a moment willing itself onto the comet but did not. There would be nothing different there than aboard the dozens of comets it had ridden. Like all comets, this one was constantly moving, its path dictated by the gravity of the bodies about it. Like all it, was beautiful and seemingly alive, although not. Like all, its heart was ice.

Wingman

On my first night in the new house,
a week after you moved out and I moved on,
after we agreed that,
however clichéd,
nothing lasts forever,
I killed a mouse.

The prior owner left the trap but it was I
who baited it with peanut butter,
found the little guy writhing,
snapped his neck with the heel of my shoe,
and dropped him trap and all into the garbage.

Then I realized
that everyone in the world
was gone;
it was only me and my mouse,
and now he was dead.
I was alone in my kitchen.

He who so loved me that he moved in
and thought to kill some time awaiting my arrival
with a bit of Jif Crunchy.
I could have called him *Skeezix* and taught him
to bring me my martini olive each night.
He could have ridden in my pocket to singles bars
and accompanied me home,
a reliable friend,
his needs, moods and responses
if nothing else
predictable.

Of course I soon came to my senses
and resumed my place as one of
Darwin's ruling class,
no longer alone in my kitchen
but an integrated part
of this teeming self-obsessed world

where you had just moved out,
I had just moved on,
and forever was over.

It was 2008 and Betty was gone and there was no sex and no beautiful child and there had been no love. Or had there? I really did not know and so I killed myself again and again. It was like whack-a-mole. Bits of me kept popping up but I was very diligent and of course I had help. There are always teachers happy to oblige.

In other words I moved to central Florida and went out on dates.

Fairy Tale

a woman

who wasn't anorexic
who wasn't addicted to sleeping pills
      who didn't have an ex-boyfriend who sold meth
      who didn't have an ex-husband still plaguing her
      who wasn't becoming someone else
      whose father did not rape her
      whose credit cards were not on overload
      who wasn't looking for her father
      who wasn't looking for an executioner
      who didn't have a string of man-pelts in her closet
      who liked sex but didn't tell everyone about it
      who wasn't desperate for a happy ending

walked into a bar with a friend

      who wasn't there to make her look good
      who didn't have man issues
      who didn't have a gun in her purse
      who didn't secretly hate her
      who didn't love her with secret lesbian yearnings
      who wasn't full of advice she couldn't take herself
      who wasn't resolved to ruin everything

and met a man

      who did not have intimacy issues
      who did not have commitment issues
      who didn't have a gun in his pocket
      whose mother didn't breast feed him until he was 8
      whose mother didn't withdraw her nipple
      whose father didn't rape him
      who wasn't just looking for sex
      who wasn't just looking to impress the guys
      who wasn't really looking for a guy
      who wasn't desperate for a happy ending
      who did not like to be tied up
      but did not rule it out, either
      who didn't think he was God's gift
      who didn't think his penis was God's gift
      who didn't think he was God

and they talked

        to each other

and they went to his place and talked some more
and did or did not make love that night
and did another night
        for the first or second time

and did not immediately decide to get married
and did not decide to hate each other
and did not fake it
        whatever it is
and did not just roll over and go to sleep
or smoke cigarettes they didn't really like
or make forcible small talk
or lie awake wondering what the hell have I done

and smiled at each other in the morning
and decided to see each other again because
        they wanted to
and didn't do what everyone said they should
or what they thought they should
or what they thought they should want
or what they wished they could want
but simply what they enjoyed
simply what seemed to be working OK

and did not drive each other crazy
and did not resign to make due
or make excuses
or make exit strategies
or just live with it
or take the bad with the good
or be disappointed
        that life wasn't perfect either

and they lived
        reasonably happily
ever after

Seconds

First of all, you are not the first of all
I am not the first of all
so we should get that out of the way, first of all.
I want to say that I really think that
it is a good thing, not being first,
because the only thing as useless as a saint
is a virgin, only there is no cure for sainthood.
Still, there are times I wish I could give you
my innocence. It is a gift given once only,
a match once lit,
and after we are first naked to each other
we will never be naked again.
Is it enough to say that if this is love
all that has come before,
was something else, something less,
some test or training or prologue,
some thing less because this love
is something to make me wonder
where I have been all my life.
I do not begrudge you your lighted fools.
We laugh over them, yours and mine,
who made us cry and now
are something less to us for it.
They may have been first, or earlier anyway,
whereas I snore and sometimes ruin the afterglow
or the pre-glow by being somewhere else in my head.
I tell you this just so you know what is wrong with me.
Because everyone knows
the key to buying seconds
is to find the flaw.

I went out on dates in Orlando, Florida, where all roads lead to Disney World. Where you only fall when you see you have run off the cliff. Because dating for some of us becomes a continuing cartoon.

Where, when your date says she believes in reincarnation or pyramid power or the violent overthrow of the government, you smile. You have heard it before and maybe that means you've been out with her before.

All of which makes sense when you speak only to yourself while you wait for someone to force you to wake up and engage.

I am fine with who I am. Who I am. I am more than any one thing. Even love. My only fear for so long was that I would disappoint you because of who I am. Because you might want grandchildren. What other use is there for a Jewish girl?

Of course you didn't marry a Jewish woman but you insisted that I be raised in your faith. Was it because you were afraid of being lonely in your own home, as you are in your own skin? Afraid of being the only Jew in the house? Weren't you afraid of being the only sober one? The only sane one? Didn't you sleep with one eye open?

I have learned in therapy that I should be proud of what I am. I have learned that anger is really just fear. That is all there is, fear and depression. We mold them into something we call happiness.

Bucket List

When I have gone from verb to noun,
my life fix-pinned like a prize moth,
the nickel eternity has loaned me repaid
(with interest I should think),

when this is it and that's that,
that's all she wrote and that's all folks,
when I am dead to all but perhaps myself,

I will have checked off
the Wailing Wall and the Eiffel Tower,
holding a child of my body,
the pain of grief and the joys of wild love,
of laughing love, whispering love,
love made with eyes wide open,
even sad love,
but I will not
have walked the moon,
seen peace danced in the streets of Jerusalem,
sat with Leonard Cohen just talking,
or heard you say *I was wrong to leave you.*

But then I suppose I will either think nothing
or be occupied with some very big things
and so I doubt I will much care
who misses me or what I am missing,
or about you or any of the other
little things I have missed.

For You Only I Will Explain My Behavior

I wake an hour before the alarm goes off,
get out of bed and make a cup of coffee,
overriding the timer.
I pad to the back porch and light a smoke
from the first pack I have purchased in 23 years.
The morning chill slips beneath my robe
as the sun rises and the tick and click of wood,
the wisp of steam from the cup, the solitary mockingbird
and the distant train promise that I will not die.

I turn on the t.v. and watch a sports show that begins
when I am due at work. I eat a bowl of sugared cereal.
I put on a polo shirt and a sportcoat so that
I will never die. At least not this morning.

I drive the long way because that way
I will not die. I close the door to my office,
check Facebook, and buy a dozen t-shirts, six ties,
an Excalibur letter opener. I download a recipe
for *pot au feu* that I will never try.
All so that I will live another day.

I send a love letter to the woman who
no longer loves me back, leave work early
and go to a movie but get up after 20 minutes
to go have one martini,
dry, up, two olives,
at an upscale bar where a faded woman looks at me,
giving me another few hours with her eyes,
and then I go drink a Bud at the dive
down the street from the dirty bookstore,
where I buy a video and drop it in the trash
as I come home, put on
Law and Order reruns
and stay up all night long.

All night.
Watching.
Keeping vigil over my life.

I have a gun. Bullets, too. How irresponsible, leaving a mess for the cleaning lady:

> "Dear Mrs. Sanchez
> I am so sorry I must leave you with this and I know it is a shock. Please call the police to cut me down. I hope I don't leave a mess under me. I hear that happens sometimes. My family has all the information they need.
>
> Thank you
> Raymond
>
> P.S. You are welcome to the leftover pork loin in the refrigerator. And I know it's very early but I left your Christmas bonus in an envelope by the dishwasher."

Razors. The thought makes the backs of my legs tingle.

Same is true for hanging, I suppose.

Poison, including sleeping pills and such, is extremely dangerous. I read that you might only pass out, throw up on yourself, aspirate and not die at all but wind up brain dead or a vegetable or something. Too horrible to imagine, having to lie there while everyone… no, too horrible to imagine.

Jumping out of a building might be OK. The ending is sudden and the trip down could actually be fun. It might be a good idea to jump from a plane over the ocean or something so there is no danger of mashing some poor devil walking under you. Then again, it is just possible that half way down you might remember that you forgot to turn off the stove.

The indignity of falling while madly flapping one's arms. No, heights are out. They scare me anyway.

I am beginning to sound like that Dorothy Parker poem.

Besides, the milk is good through Monday.

What Matters

On the morning I realized that I was dying
nothing else seemed to matter.
My wife tried to interest me in unimportant things:
our children, her feelings, the dishes,
and I just walked
away.

I went to work but sat calculating
how many years I had left
according to insurance industry actuarial averages
and then, of course, I quit because
it hardly seemed important whether
this piece of paper or that was signed,
or this number or that went into
the bank account I would only have
for another 40-odd years.

I moved to some place,
which place didn't matter.

I tried to read
but nothing seemed worth the effort;
fiction was just someone else's dreams,
some other dying person's story.
Biographies and histories were just about
people and things that happened,
science was interesting for a while, I suppose,
then even it seemed trivial.
I did not mourn the death of newspapers
because the news was hardly newsworthy;
I surfed the internet until I realized that
while it was forever, none of it made any difference.

But there was math,
and that alone seemed worth
my time, such as it was.

At first I turned away because every equation,
each marvelous secret pairing or halving,
could be nullified simply multiplying
by zero, but that was before I learned
that anything, simple or complex,
infinitely small or infinitely large,
could be divided by zero
and produce anything, everything,
nothing, something,
something else.
Something more.

As the chestnut trees in the Bronx Zoo were killed to the ground, the blight was beginning to spread
–American Chestnut History by Judy C. Treadwell
It is a wound pathogen, entering through a fresh injury in the tree's bark.
–History of the American Chestnut Foundation

ghost-grey the chestnut stands against the forest * its head is gone * no limbs strike out from its bare trunk * a hole in the side reveals * the emptiness that was tree * the morning mist renders it invisible * rain and wind * polish it * to naked beauty * to nothing * but it is the worm * that kills the American Chestnut * it is the worm within * who whispers what we are not * it is the industry of the worm to chew and poison * so that though we fall when we lose * what we love * what we are * we are already dead

Someone needs to write something for the American Chestnut. Its young grow to a certain age and then the blight takes hold. They are born with the seed of death in them.

The Flooding of Graysville

I realize that I picked the wrong time to move to Graysville, a town of 400 of which at least half are imaginary. That may not be correct, exactly. It may be that I had to be here, at least that is how it feels as I watch the citizens cross the county line that separates our home from reality.

As we walked to the edge of town, Mr. Potter, who runs the Pure station, told me part of the story. Mr. Tallent, the pharmacist, the rest. There was a flood a century ago, just like the one that is coming today. That time, there was no warning. Hundreds of people lost their lives.

When the water receded, disbelief mixed with crushing grief. Perhaps a form of denial that bordered on insanity provided a balm for the survivors. Whether that denial became palpable, someone's prayers were answered, or it was the work of a darker force than I want to imagine, what followed defies rational explanation.

The mourners found that those they lost, or others taking the places of the drowned loved ones, awoke in their beds a few weeks after the tragedy. The dead, or someone like them, or perhaps something that improved on them, came to life and walked among the living.

For generations, no one spoke of any of this. How could they? To question the return of those they mourned might end the dream. I can think of a dozen reasons why the truth was simply ignored and life, or something akin to it, went on in Graysville. Babies were conceived, born, grew old and died. People married, never questioning one another's lineage or even existence.

For all of this, Graysville and Gray County around it was the happiest place imaginable. Perhaps the ability to conjure the perfect mate, business partner or best friend remained in the soil, the rock, the air. Perhaps those who were the descendants of the unreal conformed themselves to the needs of the real. Perhaps the living developed a flexibility of character, or of need.

In the few years I have lived here, managing the small grocery store, I have come to meet many of the locals. I have always known that there was something unusual about Graysville. I have always known that I feel at home here. My past seems a dream, hazy and uncertain. This makes me uneasy because Mr. Potter and Mr. Tallent both emphasized two things when they told me the story of Graysville.

First, those of us who are not real have no idea. Everyone in Gray County recalls growing up here. They remember their families, their school years, everything. If the story of Graysville is true, these memories are as imaginary as those who keep them. Second, there is a terrible truth that is passed down by whisper through every generation. To cross the boundary of Gray County is to awake from the collective dream. Those who are real will never again experience the happiness they know in and about Graysville. Those who are not real will disappear.

And today, the waters of the Cullawasee are again overflowing. The dam constructed after the last flood is about to give way and the deadly waters that were once snow atop the surrounding mountains will crash through this valley and drown all that is now Graysville. We may choose to stay and perish or to leave. And take our chances.

Some have elected to stay. They are in their homes, or already on their roofs. The Baptist and Methodist churches are both full to capacity and we can hear hymns being sung as we crowd at the county line.

No one wants to drive out. They all want to walk. My car is broken down and, while I might be able to borrow someone's and drive away, I cannot bring myself to disrespect the people who have gathered in the drizzling rain. I find that I want to make the walk myself.

Old man Potter, shaking his head, is the first to walk out. He takes a step past the Now Leaving Gray County sign and turns around. His eyes well up with tears. Mrs. Potter passed not long after I arrived. I am not sure whether she would have made it with him, but I suppose he would have been perfectly happy had he ceased to exist. He shakes his head again, turns and trudges up the road that leads to the top of Sanctuary Mountain. For the first time I understand why it is so named.

Mayor Cason, his wife and their teenaged daughter are next. Mrs. Cason hesitates at the line, holding her daughter back. He gently pushes them on. The horror on his face as he turns to us, standing alone, is crushing. He runs back across the line, looking to his right and left, but they are gone.

Mrs. Till, who raised six sons and buried two, puts her arms around him and whispers something to him, together they walk back across the line, accompanied by her surviving sons. Two of the boys make it. I cannot watch any more of this because the pharmacist, Mr. Tallent and his wife walk solemnly to the boundary. He is an overweight, balding man of fifty and she a statuesque blonde half his age. Several of the townspeople have been unkind in whispering about how he dotes on her, treating her as much like a pet as a wife.

As they are about to cross, the Kelsey twins, Minnie and Marie, skip ahead of them. They are, as usual, giggling and as sunny as their white-blonde hair. Their parents call after them, but the girls place their toes even with the sign and then hop across. Marie's solitary, anguished wail begins as soon as her feet touch the pavement.

Mr. Tallent stops and his wife coaxes him on. He points toward town and whispers something. She shakes her head. I hear him say, "I don't know what I would do without you." To our surprise, it is he who dissolves before our eyes. She buries her face in her hands as the Kelseys run to their daughter and both make it. The Zinks are not so lucky. Both disappear. I am not sure who they leave behind, probably someone in one of the churches who does not know of their loss.

It continues all morning. We hear a siren in the distance, signaling that the dam has given way. Several people, previously unable to move, rush forward. Mr. and Mrs. Tolley and their three children and twelve grandchildren all make it but Mr. Franks and his sister-in-law Mrs. Paulson are both alone as they step across. Two spinster sisters from just outside town hold hands as they slowly walk across and one faints as she alone continues. One of our volunteer firemen, Smythe I think is his name, goes to her aid and never gets to her. Another man, whose arm is in a sling, does.

Fat, jolly Mr. Anderson, who plays Santa every year, stands at the boundary and shivers. He turns to me, his eyes imploring. I nod. He steps forward and is lost to us forever. A dozen teens, some with parents calling to them, push forward through the crowd. Two are on skateboards and sail over the line without incident, but a girl with black lipstick and nail polish and two football players pass into the air as a solitary cheerleader cartwheels over the line and then falls to her knees on the other side. She bursts into tears.

A beautiful pregnant girl, her parents on either side, steps across. Her father's eyes are on her and his expression remains stern as he disappears. The girl and her mother walk on without pause.

There are only a few of us left. The rain is coming down more heavily and I know that we may not be able to make it up the mountain even if we survive the next few steps. The secretary I have been hoping to ask out trembles as she walks across and then breaks into a run. The bartender at our only saloon bows to the barmaid and then to his mother, steps over the line and disappears. The barmaid screams and runs back into town, toward the Methodist church. The mother steps over the line and then turns around and walks back to town.

Mr. Fogle, who owns the hardware store, stands at the trunk of a tree alongside the road. He is holding onto the tree and appears frozen there. I want to go to him but it is my turn.

Someone is on my right and a woman beyond him steps forward and disappears. A child on my left, leading a puppy, gets across but I don't see her parents. Just before I walk across, I see a woman holding a baby step forward, her husband at her side. I hear her scream.

My eyes are fixed on a patch of asphalt just beyond the border between all that I think I was and all that I will or will not be. The person on my right makes it and sighs deeply. I close my eyes and step forward into a future no less uncertain than your own.

You Have Wearied the Lord With Your Words
  —Micah 2:17

heavy is the burning of the day
heavy is the solace of the night
heavy is the weight of the word
on the ear of the father

heavy the clarity of the knife
heavy the hand
and the pen
the lathe and the wheel
the wheat and the scythe
the fire
the bread
and the foot on the path

heavy the grain
the sand
the glass
the sand again

heavy is the keepsake smile
the certainty of grief
the justice of decay
the righteousness of the fall
the cruelty of iron
the truth of iron

heavy is the air in the lungs
heavy is the thought
the breath
the singer
the song

heavy is the knife with its clarity
heavy is the certainty of grief
heavy is the weight of the word on the ear
and the foot on the path
to the solace of night

I thought maybe it was because you wanted me to write poetry. Like you. So I tried. I didn't like what I wrote until I tried imagining myself someone else. By then you were older and I could imagine that we had a relationship. I could imagine I was the son you wanted. Children are born able to imagine Captain Hook and purple dinosaurs. I had to be older to imagine myself away. Then I began to write my own poetry. I never showed you.

What can we be for each other when we are merely players in one another's dreams?

They say female mammals are attracted to males who look strong and healthy. How does that explain all the women in our lives? All the Disney World dating that is at least non-threatening? I got lots of dates because I was no one and could be anyone. Does this sound familiar? I hope not. It just made me older, that is all killing time does. It does not kill time, it just makes you older without noticing. Which is how time gets back at you

I am too old for my life. I am Tithonus and I am tired. And there is much more to tell but I am tired. It just occurred to me who will read this. It will be you, won't it, Sweetheart? I am sorry. I am sorry because this is going to hurt you so much. You are the one who will read every word. Everyone else will read the first couple of sentences and shrug it off.

"Insane," they will say, "That explains everything. We always knew."

Your mom will say that. You will tell her about what I have written and she will roll her eyes. She will wonder why she isn't in the story and who the Hell Betty was. I am tired of all that. I was tired of her when I married her. I am tired of everything and every one. But never of you. You are new each time I see you. I am tired of everything else and I am…I guess tired is the only word I can come up with.

I am tired because the story about the sorcerers and thinking about what it means has kept me up so many nights of my life. I am so tired but I hope it is a good story. It is one of my favorite stories that I made up when I was very young to keep me up all the nights of my life.

At first because I was afraid of the dark and then after because I was afraid of the light. Now I am no longer afraid and that is a good thing. And it is a bad thing, isn't it?

The stories kept me awake.

The story of the sorcerers; and the story of a seven-foot tall 450 pound football player who could bench press 900 pounds but could not make people understand that being the biggest and strongest and fastest was all well and good but he was still a seven-foot tall 450 pound man and therefore a freak. Being the best means being as different as being the worst. You just don't notice it until later.

He was me. So was the vampire who was the only interesting vampire tale left to tell because he was the only vampire and hadn't the faintest idea how to make another. He could make children like everyone else, only it meant watching your wife and children die. So after a thousand years or two he gave up on that and was dreadfully lonely but he was not without hope because vampires or at least him he aged only slowly so much so that after 8752 years on this earth he was now 39 and he was looking forward to dying someday and afraid of what would happen if he did not and he just kept getting older. And he was me too of course.

How to Build a Black Hole

"Gravity is caused by the bending of space and time. So gravity is not really pulling me down to the ground. It is space that is pushing me down." Dr. Michio Kaku, CCNY.

when a star runs out of fuel it ceases to burn * when it ceases to burn gravity forces it into itself * when it turns into itself it becomes smaller denser heavier * until its own gravity will not allow even light to escape * even a star that watched the earth * form itself out of nothing * watched a wizard who spoke of things * that mattered amid things that did not * turn his staff into a snake * and magic into a name not to be said

even a star so old it should know better * will lose what makes it live and * unless someone rekindles the flame will become food for worms * until it crashes into itself pulling down * all around it

even a man pure of heart * who says his prayers by night * can fall into himself if he forgets * or loses or * gambles away * what makes him a man

Angry Men Of Our Village

Sucre buries his wife
beneath the tree where the soldier
raped and killed her
he decapitates his son and
buries him too.

Melo watches his daughter
as the fever carries her away;
he burns his house with her
still in the bed
and eats her charred hand.

Soca eviscerates his dog.
Fela his brother.
Katay cuts off his penis
and watches himself
bleed to death in the mirror
his wife left behind.

Sann spends the month
since he last worked
building a coffin for his mother,
who he stabs as she cooks
his favorite meal.

Canae wakes before dawn.
He is alone.
He yawns stretches scratches his thigh,
and hangs himself.

No Purchase In The Sky

it isn't a fear of falling falling down
it isn't a fear of falling down from some great height
from above the stars where the depth is so deep
it never ends no
it is a fear of falling up
up into that depth up into that deep emptiness when the stars
are millions in the sky and the sky is in the lake
the stars are in the lake where there is no island
to stop your eye it walks you across the starlit black water into
the starlit black sky right across there the horizon that isn't even
a razor thin break in the stars just walk straight out
and up going out and all the time you are falling up
the empty hold of the sky sucking you up
past the stars that will not break your fall up into nowhere
you see why I am so afraid while I know there is no thing to fear
I fear nothing that is what I fear the nothing if I walk
out the starlit black lake water I will fall down through the water
down and down and the stars will not hold me no purchase
in the water either I will fall as when I was a boy in my dreams
in those dreams where I have been all my life
I would dream that I was asleep and if I woke
I would fall through the ceiling and fall and fall and fall

**Appointment 10:00,
St. Vincent Office Building B,
Suite 705**

the fisherman's net is a tangle

his hat and raincoat are grey

a different grey from the sky

he must be on a boat because the shore

is behind him to his left

far away

a lighthouse is the only building

nothing moves although

so much is moving

a bowl of perfect fruit casts

its shadow across

a white cloth in the middle

of a wooden table as the sun rises

or does it set

of course I cannot be sure

it is a still life isn't that the word

still

life

still living

living still

I want something to happen

I want your diplomas to fall to the floor

I want the fisherman to drown in his net

as the lighthouse looks on

I want the fruit to rot the sun

to set rise or explode before me

anything but this not this

not the digital time on your desk

10:47
breathe

10:47

words move in the air
your hands move
time moves
but not here
10:47

you are talking

but my ears stopped at 10:46
when your kind
caring executioner's eyes
met mine
and that word from your lips
cut like a scalpel through my breast

I'm fine, Dad. That is what I said every time you asked and what I am saying to you now. It is what I will always say to you. I'm fine, just fine. I will always be fine. Whatever I am it is what I expect to be so I am just fine with it. You never gave me any reason to expect more. I expect what I have. That is how this works. You were wherever you were. I was out here, loving you, getting used to being fine. Don't ever worry about me. I am fine, I am just fine. It is who and what I am and all that I am. Fine. It is what you made me and I thank you.

To My Father Who Never Danced Anyway

Why do I fret so over my father's tortured back?
He never danced.
Walker or wheelchair or whatever it will be,
Who always waited for me to come to him.

I suppose his mind is slowed a step too,
but there is no man with whom I would rather talk
or inevitably listen;
mostly we make speeches at each other.

My mother does not understand how this is good
or that we miss each other.
We miss each other.

My father and I talk when we talk,
he at his end me at mine,
each of us at the end of the line.
He is at the end of his walking,
I the last of something else.

My father and I talk when we talk.
Perhaps we will talk in some other place
where words along with backs, legs,
any of our disappointments,
no longer confine us.

Closing Thoughts

My boy runs across the yard.
The air closes behind him.
I watch through the window.
Between us there is glass, air,
twenty-two years,
a barrier of blood.

I looked at you that way,
my reflection pale in
the pane between us.
I saw both of us more clearly
when I saw myself beside you.

People ask what keeps me going
now that so much of my life
has gone on
and my heart has closed behind it.
What keeps me going
I copied from you,
from the other side of the glass.

Soon I will leave the house
and gather up the boy.
I will stroke his head and whisper to him.
He will kiss his birth mother
and then me,
his younger mother,
pick up his toys,
try to be a mensch as I try
to give him a mensch to measure by.

These things,
your things,
I try to pass on
by word
if not by blood.

Because soon, too soon,
you will go on,
I will follow you on,
and history will close behind us.

My darling daughter,

I am so sorry but I am tired.

It will be all right. I said that to you the nights I held you and fed you your bottle and you looked at me as CNN showed the cruise missiles destroying tanks and bunkers. I knew we would be all right. You looked at me and I knew I would always protect you just like our army would save the Kuwati people and the world. I told you that it would be all right.

And so would I.
And so would you.

I am sorry but it is OK

I hope this is the only part of this letter they let you read. The rest of it was not intended for you. I don't know who I wrote it for. Maybe like the poetry it was all to please myself. Please know that I am very sorry. I know you still need me but not all that much any more and I am tired. So very tired.

Love,
Dad

This story is true the way I believe the Bible is true.
It is not what happened. It is the truth of what happened.

Does it matter if no one touched my penis when I was a little boy? That no one beat me? Do you really care whether I was or was not subjected to emotional torture? No, my mother did not withdraw her nipple. I was bottle fed because they thought it was better for me back then. My father never laid a hand on me and my parents protected me and loved me very much and I loved them. I was never abused sexually or in any other way that would make you shake your head and say, "Poor him!"

So what?
This is a poem, anyway.
Does it matter that
this poem is not about me?
Nothing is about me.
This is not about me,
but it is true.
And it is fiction.
It is love and it is abuse.
It is fun and it is scary.
It is not a poem because it is prose.
It is neither and both because it is a letter.
Every poem is a love poem
and every letter is a confession and every touch
no matter how intended is a confession is abuse is loving.

Don't worry about me, whoever you are reading this..
It is OK.
It is OK because it is where
I have been for a very long time.
It is OK because it is true.

This letter is true because this letter is my life.
And now it is done.

R. S.

False Spring

and at night you think you see

they have appeared from a dream

at the side of the road

they watch bewildered

your headlights sweep over

the impossibly graceful necks

the soft faces delicate legs

what if one bolts into your path

what if you are not quick enough

what if your daughter is in the back

what is it daddy what happened

will it be all right

legs scissoring across the asphalt

ragged night breathing

the naked eye staring into you

wanting to believe that you are not wolf

that day will follow night

that the world is good

that your hand will not slip

Raymond L. Shaw, of Coconut Grove, Florida, passed away on February 24, 2013. Mr. Shaw was survived by his loving daughter, L. Shopinski, of Ontario, Canada. He was a partner in the insurance firm of Weismann, Goldberg & Shaw. Mr. Shaw was a graduate of the University of Miami, where he received a degree in English, with honors. Services were held at graveside at the Greater Miami Jewish Cemetery, 1125 N.W. 137th Street, and were attended by Mr. Shaw's family. The family asks that donations in Mr. Shaw's honor be made to the University of Miami Suicide Prevention Resource Center.

The Miami Herald | Wednesday, February 28, 2013

AFTERWORD - MY PAGE

If I had one more thing to say to him, it would be this:

Twenty-something years of therapy. Twenty-something years of talking to this person and that about this and that and over and over about mom. Always mom. Sometimes about you, but always about mom.

I wonder what it would have been like if Freud hated his father instead of his mother?

I could hate you for this. I did once. To be honest, maybe I never forgave you, only burned out. The probing about Tommy and why I think the boys picked me and yes, they probably sensed that I was different and not interested in their dull little penises and yes, I knew, I always knew and no, I hadn't started masturbating to Playtex bra ads and yes these questions are another form of …violation.

That's a tired metaphor, isn't it, Dad?

Why don't they want to know about you? About being told that I was supposed to bring another little Shaw (nee Shopinski) into the world. You could hide behind the Christian name that Great-Great-Grandad took when he hit Ellis Island, not that it did any good for the family who stayed in Poland. You could boff every shiksha waitress in the Grove, but I had to remember my role. I am a link in a chain, like you said at my Bat Mitzvah. I am here to add another link. Another future candidate for the therapeutic process created by a self-hating Viennese Jew with an oral fixation and a mother who must have been Hell on Wheels. Like mom.

Like Mrs. Rubenstein, who taught me piano and a whole lot more. Like Suzie, my college roommate and Toni and the other LUGs at Agnes Scott. But not like Janie, the mother of my child. You never met her. I am truly sorry for that.

I can talk to you about this now. You don't have a door to close. By the way, I love you.

L. S.

L. Shopinski is a freelance writer and author of two short story collections, *Portrait of the Artist* (Ontario Press, 2008), which was a finalist for the Canadian New Author's Prize, and *The Dragon's Tale* (Broken Wing Press, 2010), which was named Book of the Year by the Tri-State Short Story Guild. Her children's book, *It Isn't In the Closet* (Tinker Toy Press, 2011) won a Caldecott Award. She is the winner of two Pushcart Prizes and an O. Henry Award. Ms. Shopinski and her partner live in Ontario, Canada, with their son. She is working on a novel set in Poland before the Second World War.

AFTERWORD

I am not Raymond Shaw.

None of my children is L.

Only my children can say if they are L.

Only my children can say if I am Raymond Shaw.

Everyone is Raymond Shaw.

Raymond Shaw is a fictional character.

This is like dividing by zero.

In third grade, Ms. Parker explained that you cannot divide by zero.

Because every answer will be right.

And therefore none of them will be right.

I never got over it.

My parents never explained it to me.

Many parents are too busy for their children.

They say they are busy with work.

The truth is we are too busy with ourselves.

That is a cliché.

The worst thing about clichés is that they do not communicate.

They do not communicate because they turn off the mind.

We say, "I heard that one before. Tell me something new."

I want to tell you a story.

I have tried to tell it in a way that is not a cliché.

I want it to be the truth.

The common definition of truth is that it is factually accurate.

There is no narrative voice-over for our lives.

We experience life by sensory perception and emotion.

We describe it by recounting facts.

We think facts make a story true.

I think there is more to a story than the facts.

I want you to understand more than the story.

I want you to understand me and those like me.

I value my privacy over everything else.

I value my children over everything else.

You are no different from me.

You are unique.

Some of the poems in this book are intended to be funny.

They were written when I was severely depressed.

The Muse works that way.

Go figure.

I hope you enjoyed my book.

I hope you are a person who does not understand what I am saying.

I would say God Bless you but that might offend you.

That is absurd.

It is absurd to be afraid to say "God."

It is absurd to seek the true religion.

All religions are the true religion.

It is like dividing by zero.

Life is absurd.

I hope you are a person who understands that life is absurd.

God Bless You.

BSM

Barry Marks is a Birmingham attorney, and the author of two books of poetry. *Possible Crocodiles,* his first book, was named 2010 Book of the Year by the Alabama State Poetry Society. *Sounding,* his second book, is an emotional but unsentimental examination of grief, loss and recovery. *Sounding* was a finalist for the Grand Prize in the 2013 Eric Hoffer Award for Independent Publishers Competition. He is former a member of the Big Table Poets and has participated in that group's anthologies. Barry's chapbook, There is Nothing Oppressive as a Good Man, won the 2003 John and Miriam Morris Chapbook Competition. Barry was Alabama's Poet of the Year for 1999 and is a frequent reader, lecturer and workshop leader.

INDEX TO POEMS & STORIES

An Epiphany	16
Appointment 10:00 St. Vincents Office Building B, Suite 705	70
"As Hell"	37
A Dream Story	20
All the Robin Hoods Meet in Sherwood Forest	5
Angry Men of Our Village	68
Bucket List	56
Closing Thoughts	73
Depression	50
Doc Holliday Says Goodbye to Wyatt Earp	39
Fairy Tale	53
False Spring	76
Flying In Bed On Sunday Morning	44
For You Only I Will Explain My Behavior	57
Fordham Evers Kidnapped A Busload Of Tourists On Their Way To The Top Of Mount Early	24
Fred Didn't Want to Have Sex	48
I Can't Help It	10
I Remember That an Angel Made Me Forget	9

I Saw Death In Your Backseat	32
I Woke With A Dream Of Your Father	47
Komodo	40
Little Match Girl	28
My Wife Marvels At My Hunting Knife Before the Brownie Camping Trip	36
No Purchase in the Sky	69
Ode to My Daughter's Cat	7
Portrait of the Artist	17
Seconds	55
Titanic Dreams	21
The Flooding of Graysville	61
The Fuller Brush Man Doesn't Stop Here Anymore	15
To My Atheist	14
To My Father Who Never Danced Anyway	72
Watching a Nature Show I Get Close to My Inner Mammal	13
What Death is This?	22
What Matters	59
When Asked What I Think about Death I Remember The Truck	1
Wingman	51
You Have Wearied the Lord With Your Words	65
Your Body Your Body	43